*This book is dedicated to the ı
men who struggle to get appoıɴʈ·ᴍᴇʀɪᴛᴜ ·ᴀ··ᴅ ·ᴜ·
those leads and appointments into new clients.*

*The strategies and tips shared here are proven by
me and many of my clients. There are no sales
gimmicks, slick tricks, or black hat ideas that don't
work or leave you and your prospect feeling icky.*

Not interested in speaking to groups? No problem!

These principles and skills work beautifully in
- *Blog posts*
- *Articles*
- *Email campaigns*
- *Networking events*
- *1-on-1 appointments*

*When you apply and master the strategies in this
book, you'll be able to fill your appointment calendar
easier and faster than ever before!*

*Are you ready to finally having the success, income,
and life you always dreamed about?*

Table of Contents

Chapter 1: Sue's Story

I went to a small school in a rural community. Grades 7-12 were all in the same building. I remember distinctly the time the school hired a speaker to address the students.

The speaker was dynamic! I don't remember what the topic was but I remember being mesmerized by his presence. His stories were engaging, his delivery had us leaning forward so we'd catch every single word. Even the 7th and 8th grade boys sat still and paid attention!

I remember thinking to myself, "I want to be like that!" I wanted to be a person who could influence change and motivate others to be more and do more. I didn't know how or when it was going to happen, but someday, somehow, it would. I was sure of it.

My first attempt to be in front of a group and be an "influencer" came with our school play auditions. I tried out and got a secondary role. I practiced. I sweated. I lost sleep. I threw up. I memorized. I practiced in front of a mirror. I was terrified! And the night of the play, I froze. I forgot every single line. I was a major failure and an embarrassment to the other students in the play. My first and last attempt as an actress!

A couple of years later I was part of an organization, Future Homemakers of America (FHA). Before you get upset, this was back in the early '70's and being a "homemaker" wasn't ridiculed. FHA had been asked to activate their group of young women to write down codes on the top of baby food jars from local grocery stores and submit them to their agency.

At that time, expiration dates weren't marked and shoppers had no idea on the quality of what they were buying and feeding their babies. This group was working to get legislation passed on labeling all baby food with clearly marked expiration dates.

Somehow, I was chosen to go from my little town in SE Minnesota to Los Angeles and report our findings from the stage at the Biltmore Hotel. It was a big deal. I got a couple of new dresses, a new haircut, and my first suitcase.

I had notes so the delivery went fine. I was passionate about sharing the story of the mom I'd watched open a jar of baby food, dab her finger in the jar, taste it, replace the lid, and put it back on the shelf. My passion dulled the fear plus it had been a couple of years since the school play debacle, so I had matured a little. And I'd taken a speech class which helped dramatically – the teacher was phenomenal!

After we were done speaking, the press lined up chairs for a photo op. The chair backs were a few inches from the end of the stage. We were to be seated with our backs to the audience so the full auditorium could be seen behind us in the photo.

Now, grace has never been my middle name. This was in the early 70's where mini-skirts reigned. As I sat down in the chair assigned to me, I ended up moving the chair and back legs slid off the stage, the chair and I crashed onto the floor below, head over heels.

When people rushed up to me to ask if I was ok, the only thing that came out of my mouth was, "Did my underwear show?" Of course it did! I was wearing a miniskirt!

<u>I was mortified and decided right then and there that I was NOT cut out to be a speaker.</u>

But decades later, the desire became so strong that I had to find a way to make it happen. How could I build a speaking career with 6 kids and while operating our organic dairy farm in the middle of nowhere?

It was an interesting path and I'll be sharing stories about this journey with you throughout the book. My journey will help you understand what to do and, of course, what to avoid!

What's happened since I started speaking professionally in 2009? Why am I qualified to write this book?

- More than 5,000 people from 20 countries have taken my *"Social Media Marketing Success in Just 15 Minutes a Day"*.

- More than 8,000 people have attended some type of training I've done, which includes:

    - 10-minute mini-trainings on networking for profits
    - 20 and 30-minute workshop to organizations and associations,
    - Leadership training to BNI members throughout our region, (Business Network Int'l)
    - 45-minute keynotes to companies, organizations, associations, and corporations

- o 2 hour intense trainings
- o Being a guest of others on webinars, podcasts, and telesummits.
- o Being an panel expert at a number of events

I've also had the opportunity to be a contributing author is several books.

- o **"Masters of Sales"** by Ivan Misner (Founder of BNI) was a #1 NY Times, Wall Street Journal, and Business Week bestseller *(included other contributing authors Jack Canfield, Oprah, Tony Robbins, Zig Ziglar, and many others)*
- o **"World's Worst Networker"** by Tim Houston, an Amazon bestseller
- o **"Understanding, Leveraging, & Maximizing LinkedIn"** by Neal Schaffer. My company is used a case study for how I monetized LinkedIn to get a speaking gig)

Why am I telling you all this? (Besides giving you a good laugh?)

I believe we are here to make a difference in the lives of others. We each have gifts, talents, abilities, and skills that will can help us lift and serve others. Our dreams can be accomplished even if we occasionally forget our lines or fall off the stage!

You are here because YOU are important. Other people want and need what you offer. The drive to help them is inside your heart, mind, and soul.

The purpose of this book is to help you to develop the skills necessary to obtaining more appointments with hot prospects whether you are meeting them at networking events, conferences or workshops, if they call you looking for information, or if you talk to groups consisting of your target market.

These principles and skills work beautifully in blog posts, articles, and email campaigns. When you apply and master the strategies in this book, you'll be able to fill your appointment calendar easier and faster than ever before!

Be courageous, my friend. I promise the journey will be worth it.

And, should you get stuck or need help, simply go to my online calendar and book a FREE 30-minute strategy session. This IS NOT a 30-minute pitch session!

During our time together I'll ask you a number of questions and share a few ideas based on your specific business and goals. Around minute 28 into our 30 minute call I'll ask you you want my help with any of the strategies we discussed. Easy peasy.

No pressure. No obligation. No pitch-slapping.

http://timetrade.com/book/D58FP

Chapter 2: Facts Tell But Stories Sell

People want good information but they want entertainment as well. We live in a world of interactive gamification… the most successful products engage the buyer with some type of emotional experience.

As business professionals, we need to model this strategy. We want our prospects to lean forward as we talk and think, *"This is exactly what I need. I'm so glad I'm here!"*

How do we accomplish this? By sharing interesting, relevant stories that make our point. **Facts tell but stories sell!** The highest paid professionals in many fields are those who have mastered the art of storytelling.

Our grandparents and parents shared stories about their lives that became part of who we are. We share those stories as well as our own with our family. We read stories to our children, watch stories on the movie screen, and read stories (novels, short stories) as entertainment. Jesus used stories (parables) to teach important principles.

Becoming a great storyteller will help you reach, engage, and compel your prospect to take action. Stories are all around us. Watching and listening to people and situations around us will provide the foundation for many stories. We can "tweak" them to suit our needs.

Let me share an example. Julie, a life insurance agent, called me and asked for help. She was presenting to her local American Business Women Association (ABWA) members and knew that most life insurance presentations are a huge YAWN for the audience.

From previous experience, she knew that the minute she pulled up charts and graphs, her prospects' eyes would glaze over, they'd lose interest and they'd look around for the nearest exit or grab their phone to check messages, Facebook, etc.

After a few questions and a short phone conversation with Julie, I was intrigued. Julie wasn't the stereotypical life insurance sales person. She was in her mid-30's, never married, no kids.

I asked her why she became a life insurance agent. She shared: *"When I was 10, my mom died after a long battle with cancer. Because they had life insurance, we were able to stay living in the house. It really made a difference to our family."*

We worked together to transform her factual explanation into an emotionally engaging story that would bring tears to the eyes of those she shared it with because <u>they felt the story.</u>

I asked additional questions and we expanded her story to this:

When I was 10 years old, my mom died after a long battle with cancer. We knew it was coming but it didn't make saying goodbye to her any easier.

After the funeral, we came home. My brother and I each went into our own rooms. I was sitting on the bed, so incredibly sad, and thought that if dad held me for a little while, maybe I would feel better.

I left my room and as I walked down the hall, I could hear dad and his parents talking in the kitchen. My grampa said "Son, if you and the kids need to move in with us for a while until everything is settled and the house is sold, you are welcome to stay as long as you need to."

My heart stopped… What? What did he say? No!!! We couldn't sell the house. I mean, this is the bedroom where my mom would read to me when couldn't get out of bed… and when she was too weak to read to me, I'd read to her!

And this is the kitchen where we made cookies and created memories before she became so ill!

I was just about to run into the kitchen and scream,"No! You can't sell this house!" when my dad told his parents, "It's ok. Several years ago Kathy and I bought life insurance. There is enough to pay off the mortgage, pay off the medical bills, and still have some to put aside for the kids' college funds."

She ended with, "That's why I sell life insurance."

Pretty powerful, right? This same technique can be done with any story. And stories are everywhere around us!

One great place to find stories is from your customers. Examine their problem and the results they experienced after you helped them.

Is the pain similar to the pain that your ideal prospects are experiencing?

Are they searching for an answer from someone they can trust?

What story can you develop and use that will capture their interest, give them hope that there is a solution, and then gently motivate them to respond to your call of action?

Use first names in your story, even if you change them. It adds much more credibility than merely stating "one of my customers".

Another benefit to using stories is that <u>you aren't restricted, even if you're in a highly regulated industry</u>! You aren't sharing facts, statistics, etc. You are simply sharing a story and the results that person experienced without any promise. The words you use when you emotionally engage the prospect is what helps that person put themselves in the story and "feel" the results the person in your story experienced.

When story ideas come to your mind, jot them down. I always have my phone with me so I jot down just enough to spark my memory in Evernote. (more on that later)

Stories are not sales "pitches", but an engaging way to interact with the person you are talking to, Build on the situations they are experiencing, and bring them to a logical conclusion that makes them want to become your customer.

Looking for help in creating your first powerful story?

Simply go to my online calendar and book a FREE 30-minute strategy session. **This IS NOT a 30-minute pitch session!**

During our time together I'll ask you a number of questions and share a few ideas based on your specific business and goals. Around minute 28 into our 30 minute call I'll ask you you want my help with any of the strategies we discussed.

Easy peasy. No pressure. No obligation. No pitch-slapping.

http://timetrade.com/book/D58FP

Chapter 3 – Who & Where Is Your Target Market

Not all events are created equal! You want to attend the events or speak to groups that are filled with YOUR target market.

First of all, let's get clear on who your target market is. In a nutshell, they should want, need, be willing to buy AND have the money to buy what you offer!

If someone's pain is strong enough, they will figure out a way to pay for what you offer. Don't make the buying decision for them.

Identify the top 3 clients you would love to clone.
1. What was their big pain?
2. What problems was this causing them?
3. Why did they reach out for help?
4. How did they find you?
5. How did you help them?
6. How did the solution help their business?
7. How did the solution help their life?

Let's do a little research to figure out where they are.

First of all, find out what clubs, associations, and organizations meet in your community Local libraries often have a list of all the different groups that meet, giving date, time, location and sometimes a contact name, phone number, and email.

Once you have the list, decide which ones seem relevant to what you want to accomplish.

Do some online research..

1. Can guests visit before becoming a member?
2. Do they have speakers?
3. Are there professional requirements?
4. How often are the meetings?
5. How long are the meetings?
6. Is there a charge?

Next, go to LinkedIn and search for the name of the group. Who shows up that is either a first or second connection to you?

If it's someone you know personally, it's easier to contact them and ask if you can attend as their guest or how they go about bringing in speakers to the group (if you want to speak to the group).

If you don't know anyone, connect with someone who seems to be very involved and ask them for more information. Often this will lead to they asking if you'd like to be their guest.

If you are interested in speaking to the group, ask a member of the group who the program director is and request a warm introduction.

Where does your target market hang out? LinkedIn is a great research resource.

1. What local networking groups do they attend? (Business chambers, Rotary, service clubs)
2. What professional organizations do they belong to? Is there a chapter that meets locally?

3. What other organizations or associations would your target market belong to? Do these have local meetings?
4. Are they active with their alma mater and alumni groups?
5. Are there local "Meet Up" groups which attract your target market?
6. Where do they hang out online?

Another great way to connect with your target market is to ask your current and past customers/clients/patients what groups they belong to.

If you want to speak to their group, ask if they know the program director and if they'd be willing to recommend you. I suggest you get the recommendation in writing to include with your proposal request.

The more you understand about the group, their mission, culture, and purpose, the easier it will be to emphasis those points in your initial conversation, 1-sheet, proposal, and your actual presentation. Keep it about them.

Once you know which groups to connect with and what their "hot buttons" are, it's time to meet them and build your business.

If you are struggling to identify your ideal target prospects, reach out and schedule a free 30-minute consult with me. http://timetrade.com/book/D58FP

I'm going to be honest - If you want to build your business faster than you can imagine, learn how to speak to groups that are filled with your target market.

Here are some benefits to speaking for free:

1. Someone else has gotten your prospects into the room to listen to you.

2. You can share points from your compelling offer to capture the attention of the audience and keep them in the palm of your hand.

3. You can use a simple hand out with a form that asks if they'd like to sign up for your free report. They fill in their name and email and return to you before leaving the event. You leave with a pocket full of people who want more about what you shared.

4. They are automatically added to your list (because your free report requires an opt-in) and now they are part of the email campaign you'll learn how to design later in this book.

5. You also offer a free, 30-minute free strategy session on this form that some people sign up for. Now you have people to call right away *because they asked you to!*

Here's why I love speaking for free for groups that are filled with my target market:

If the room has 40 ideal prospects, a 40-minute talk will generate between $6,000-$8,000 over the next two months based on the calls I return and my email campaign. That's on a $500 product and doesn't include any upsells, etc.

Although networking is great and I love meeting new people, it just doesn't give me the same return on time investment that speaking does.

If you'd like to learn more how to speak to groups, even if you are timid, shy, and introverted, schedule a free 30-minute strategy session with me. No pressure. No obligation. But you just might be surprised at how easy this could be...

And there are over 7,000 speaking gigs in the US every single day!!! Imagine the possibilities!

Chapter 4: Create A Stampede Of Hot Prospects Begging For More Information

When you go to networking events, do you go to buy something? Or become someone's new prospect?

Of course not! And neither does anyone else!

When you speak at events, do you want to be one of those high-pressure sales people who makes everyone feel uncomfortable? Or do you skip any kind of call-to-action because you don't want to seem pushy?

Sure, you may get a sweet new client every now and then this way but it's not a sustainable business model for prospecting and building your business. That's why we are going to approach it differently...

First of all, let's determine what action you want a prospect to take whether it's a casual conversation, appointment with a prospect or speaking to a group.

I highly recommend that your offer has **high value in THEIR opinion** and is **FREE.**.

Talk in benefits, not features. What's in it for them?
1. Increased Profits?
2. Efficiency and getting more done in less time?
3. More sales, higher closing ratio, and/or repeat or upsell sales?
4. Time management?
5. How is this information going to impact their business?

Begin by creating a Compelling Offer of 10-15 tips. Each tip is 2-3 sentences with one suggestion and general information. Your total report should be 2 pages, 3 at the most. You want to share enough to whet their appetite but not give away your secret sauce.

For example, my free compelling offer is *"Top 15 Tips To Speak Your Way To Success"*. There are 15 tips and each one is only a couple of sentences. In my talks, I expand on 3 of the tips in a way that provides great content, engages them emotionally, helps them "see" themselves with successful results, and entices them to know to know more.

It's easy to pull out one of these tips and use it when:
1. I talk with people at networking events,
2. Chat on the phone with prospects
3. Writing a blog post, article, or status update
4. Create email campaigns
5. Running paid advertising or FB page promotion
6. As a guest on podcasts or radio shows

Choose **3-4** tips from your report as your "go-to" ideas. If you truly know your target market, you'll know which ones are their "hot" buttons. The goal is to choose tips that will resonate with at least 75% of your ideal prospects.

In marketing, (blog, website, sales letter, video, podcast, YouTube, etc.), you need to capture the person's attention in the first 5-7 seconds. <u>You need to recapture their attention every couple of minutes</u> People have been conditioned (through marketing, video games, etc.) to quickly jump to the next thing.

This also <u>applies to speaking</u>. You have a few seconds to capture their attention. Within 10 seconds your audience will decide if they think you are credible and worth listening to. Once you capture their attention, you need to make sure you recapture it again with each new item you are talking about.

Think for a minute about a fire hose, a kitchen faucet, and a shot glass. If I wanted to fill the shot glass with water, what would happen if I used a fire hose? Or the kitchen faucet turned on all the way? It would make a huge mess and the force from the water pressure would actually blow the water out of the shot glass. However, if I turned on the faucet to just a trickle, the shot glass would become full without spraying water everywhere.

<u>Be the faucet that trickles information to your audience, not the fire hose that forces so much information on them that they walk away overwhelmed and paralyzed</u>!

Have the link for your free report added to the back of your business card. This makes it easy for you to share the link when you are talking to an interested prospect plus it gives them a reason to keep the card.

I strongly recommend you have the free report set up on an autoresponder so the person has to opt in with their name and email address in order to access the information. This lets you know who signed up so you can reach out and begin building rapport and credibility.

Your free offer needs to be high-quality content. Their opinion of you, your company, and what you can bring to the table will be determined by the quality of your free offer.

The free offer also separates the people who are interested from the "tire kickers". Now you can spend your time with the people who are more serious about what you offer.

Sign up on the link below to see my report that you can model yours after. *"Top 15 Tips To Speak Your Way To Success"*, http://suehenrytalks.com/top-15-tips-optin/

Chapter 5: Sell Without Pitching

Although the main example here is for business professionals who want to speak to a room filled with their ideal prospects, this same strategy applies to networking, newsletters, and email campaigns.

Does this sound familiar?

You meet people at an event and they seemed really interested in what you shared. They said they were going to call you to schedule an appointment.

Or...

You speak at an event. You know you were at the top of your game! The audience loved you and people came up to you afterward, asking for your card or information. You are excited because of all the interest. Sales are going to start rolling in!

A few days pass. A few more days go by. Nothing. Weeks pass. Nothing.

You are frustrated – *What happened to all those people who were going to touch base with you?*

Life happened. You see, they walk out of the room with the best of intentions. But life smacks them alongside the head when they walk back to their car. They check their phone and start responding to voice messages. They get to the office and respond to more messages and emails. Then they tackle the work that piled up since they were gone.

They put your information on a corner of their desk thinking, "I'll touch base later this week when I get caught up."

Days and weeks go by. Your information is still there but the energy and enthusiasm has waned. They may feel a little silly calling after so long. So they toss your info in the trash.

But it doesn't have to be this way! That's why I've written this book – so you don't rely on luck or leave your fate (and income) in the hands of others. It's time to take control!!!!

Bob Burg, in his book**, Adversaries Into Allies: Win People Over Without Manipulation or Coercion"** he explains that "*selling is about moving others to accept our ideas…*" It's about influence. And he describes the Ultimate Influence as *"the ability to get the results you want from others while making them feel genuinely good about themselves, the process, and about you."*

This is why I coach my clients to have a "compelling offer". I covered this in the previous chapter but as a reminder, it's usually 2-3 pages in length and covers the "what", not the "how". (The "how" is what they pay you for!)

For example, my compelling offer is "Top 15 Tips To Speak Your Way To Success". Anyone who reads this will glean a couple of ideas he or she hadn't considered before. Each tip is 2-3 sentences. It's long enough to share my idea but not so long as it explains exactly how to accomplish or achieve the end result.

There is enough information to whet the appetite of the reader and begin building rapport.

You can offer this free report to the person (or audience) you are talking to and with their permission, opt them in. Do not wait for them to take action – take control of your future by following this step:

Create a sales funnel or process with the products and services you offer. Then develop an intentional process to move them through your system. My favorite tool for all of this is ClickFunnels. *(I'll share more about it in the resources section. I use this for my sales & thank you pages, lead capture, and membership site where my online course is accessed).*

Your goal is to lead your prospects from one item to the next, least expensive to most expensive. Let them choose the one that works best for them – don't filter what you offer from where YOU are in life!

People buy when they want to buy, not when we want them to buy!

One of my clients was afraid to charge $2497 for a 1-day intensive VIP day because she wasn't at a point in her business where she could afford to spend that kind of money herself. She was allowing her circumstances to dictate her offerings.

We worked through her mindset and she added it to her funnel. She was thrilled when a client actually purchased the offer to work with her one-on-one! If you don't ask, the answer is always "NO"!

Tip: The more 1:1 time with you, the more expensive the product/service should be.

The goal is to create a lot of value when talking about your compelling offer so people will say "Yes, sign me up!{

Here are some interesting statistics about our prospects:

1. 3% are actively shopping RIGHT NOW for what you offer
2. 7% are open if it showed up in front of them - but they aren't actively searching
3. 30% want what you offer but it's on the back burner. No urgency.
4. 30% don't even know they have the problem
5. 30% will never be interested so bless and release them

Most business professionals and speakers focus on the 3% who are "hot" for an immediate sale. But they ignore the remaining 67%. That's a lot of money, and profits, being left on the table!

That's why we create the free compelling offer! It allows you to:

1. Marketing directly to the 10% who want what you offer
2. Create urgency for the 30% who were thinking "Later"
3. Introduce the problem, solution, and results to the 30% who didn't even know they had a problem until they heard you speak

My method allows you to "sell without selling" to 70% of the people you meet WITHOUT PITCH-SLAPPING them!

Will they all buy right now? No. If you follow my system, you should see a large portion of your sales between your 5th and 12th email in the 14-email sequence. If you follow my system and create powerful stories in your campaign, this should generate sales over the next 8 weeks.

When you sprinkle your networking efforts, speaking opportunities, blog posts, and social media posts with a free offer the audience wants, they will give their contact information to you in exchange. This puts you in the driver's seat of your business and income.

Instead of waiting and hoping that they will call you, take control. Have them fill out a form and give it to you. Then you (or your assistant) will add them to your sequence of automated and strategic messages that engage them emotionally and offer the logic they need to justify buying.

With a little tweaking and experience, you'll create a sales generating machine!

Chapter 6: Emails That Convert!

I'm going to warn you right now – this is the hardest section to build for most people. Although I work 1-on-1 with my private clients to edit and help write their email sequence, it still takes at least 4-5 sessions to get through all of this. So cut yourself some slack... you aren't going to be able to roll this out on a raining afternoon.

But... once done, it can be used for several years without having to rewrite or retweak the content. How sweet is that???

Do it once and let it continue to convert your list of prospects into buyers!!!!

The purpose of our emails is to generate sales. You will want to include some type of call-to-action in most of them. These can be as easy as referring the reader to a blog post or giving them the link to your online calendar and ask them to schedule an appointment.

There are only 2 reasons why people won't buy from you:

1. They don't want or need it
2. They don't trust you enough to buy it from you

Your email sequence has 4 distinct roles:

1. Position yourself different than your competition. Show value in your content and posture yourself as a "celebrity" in your field.

2. Remind people of the pain they are in because of their problem. Make them "feel" the pain through stories and examples.
3. Give them relief by sharing the results people have gotten and how it's made a difference in their lives.
4. Demonstrate that you can actually help them get what they want and let them know how. Think of it in these terms: people don't buy glasses, they buy vision.

All of these emails are based upon honesty, integrity, and building good will with our prospects and current consumers.

There are several elements you'll want to include to increase your conversions. These are:

1. Choose what you want to sell from your funnel.
2. Write great headlines. What can you write in the subject line to increase your open rates? Here are a couple of ways to find great, attention-getting headlines:
a. **http://www.magazines.com** Search for the magazines in your industry and study the cover for the headlines they use.
b. Go to Amazon and look for books in your industry. Read through the chapter headings in the Table of Contents. What jumps out at you? There are no copyrights on titles so you can swipe and adapt to your emails.
c. Go to **http://www.technorati.com** This is an index for blogs. Find the most popular blogs in your industry and study what headlines they are using that get the most comments and engagement. Swipe and adapt for your emails.

3. Have a list of benefits (emotional) and features (logical) of what you are offering. People buy based on emotion but rationalize the purchase with logic.
4. Write down 3 questions you are most commonly asked
5. Write down 3 questions people should ask but don't know enough to ask
6. Have a swipe file of customer testimonials. I like to use the person's first name and just first initial of their last name. There is no reason to include both names. One of the easiest ways to obtain these testimonials is to (a) email the client and explain what you want and why, and (b) use your smart phone and ask if you can video their 15-20 second testimonial. Be sure to include the person's name under the video when you post it.
7. What can you offer for free to "sweeten the pot" and really make your list feel that you care? Is there a free ebook you came across that is congruent with your offer? A free checklist? Podcast?
8. Let YOU come out. Weave parts of who you are throughout your communication. For instance, we are organic dairy farmers. I often use farm or cow stories to illustrate a point. My target market is not dairy farmers yet they love the stories and the "lesson" at the end. You may think your life is boring but others may find it fascinating.

Let's get started on the 14-Email Sequence:

Email 1: This is your "thank you for opting in page". Create a custom thank you page and include the link for the information you requested. This starts building trust immediately because they can easily access the info.

Email 2: Create anticipation. Talk a little about your product or service. With bullets, highlight 3 features and 3 benefits. Appeal to the emotional and logical triggers. Add a short story about how some people have trouble delivering the solutions promised. But you don't because _____ (you have a proven system or something that you know you excel at). Add a teaser and let them know you'll be providing a solution in the next email so be sure watch for it!

Email 3: What do you have the juiciest, most emotionally-charged and dramatic results story about? Share the story – make them feel like they are a part of the story! Then share the solution. Invite them to read more and provide a link to your sales page.

Email 4: What are the 3 most common questions people ask you about the problem you solve? Then provide a short response for each. Focus on the "what" and not the "how". They pay you for the "how".

Email 5: Send 3-4 testimonials from clients. All you need is their first name and the first initial of their last name. If you have a video testimonial, provide the link but also have it written out.

Email 6: What are the questions your prospects should be asking but don't know enough to ask? Provide a short response for each. Focus on the "what" and not the "how". They pay you for the "how". Invite them to your sales page by providing a link.

Email 7: Create a 4 P's piece. In marketing, this is known as the Promise, Picture, Proof, and Push method. State your promise, help them picture the results they'll experience, provide proof through stats or testimonials, and then push them to take action now.

Email 8: Talk about why you got into the business. Share your passion.

Email 9: Share another success story of someone who used your product, the results they got, and how it affected their life. Bring in emotion! Dig that spoon in the rib cage so they feel the pain. When you share the results and how the person's life was better, that's like applying an icepack to the bruise.

Email 10: Send three more customer testimonials. Invite them to your sales page by providing a link.

Email 11: Offer a special bonus with a deadline that has value in THEIR eyes if they buy within a certain time frame. Set a deadline and hold to it.

Email 12: Resend Email 7 with a different story. Include your promise, help them picture the results they'll experience, provide proof through stats or testimonials, and then push them to take action now.

Email 13: Share another success story. Thank them for reading your messages and let them know that the bonus will be expiring within ___ days. Include the link to the sales page.

<u>Email 14:</u> The final in your series. The bonus has expired. You hope that they enjoyed and learned from your messages and when the time is right, you've laid the foundation for them to come to you for help.

You may want to find a partner to write your emails with. This person can help you understand if the story and lesson are easy to understand, if what you are sharing is compelling, and last but not least, check for typos and other errors.

If writing is a struggle for you and you are committed to creating a strategic method for converting leads to paying clients, reach out and schedule a free 30-minute strategy session with me. I'll share 2-4 tips that will help you move forward. No pressure. No obligation.

Click here for my online calendar: http://timetrade.com/book/D58FP

Chapter 7: Referral Magic!

This chapter is devoted to finding referrals for ideal prospects or speaking gigs from your warm market.

Referral partners. Identify these people, build relationships, and ask if they'd be willing to promote you to their list of prospects and clients. Referral partners fall into 3 main categories:

1. Who serves the same target market but for a non-competing product or service?
2. Who serves your ideal client first before they would need/want what you offer?
3. Who does your ideal client go to for advice on how to find you?

Clients and customers. For some reason, we seem to believe that if we do a good enough job, our clients, customers and/or patients will automatically refer us to others. But that's not reality.

If you would like to be consciously referred by your clients and customers, here are 3 ways you can approach them:

1. Ask for their testimonial in writing and for permission to put on your website and marketing materials. If they are in business, be sure to mention that you'll be adding their business name. Grab a photo of the person (not the business or sign) to use. Studies show that testimonials with a person's face are seen as more "credible" than those without.

2. Ask for a video testimonial using the same principles as above.
3. Create a reward program
4. Send them a template with a couple of sentences that state what you do, who you do it for, and the problem you solve. Then ask if they would write a warm introduction above your content and then send it to their list.

Online connections – especially LinkedIn! Sort by industry so you can focus your attention on those industries you've already had success with.
1. Who are you connected to? Why?
2. What do you have in common?
3. What groups do they belong to?
4. Join 3 new groups that are filled with your target market. Pay attention to the conversations and add suggestions and ideas when appropriate. Although you can't "pitch" in these groups without getting kicked out, you can begin to build credibility and set yourself up as an expert.
5. Start your own group and invite your ideal prospects. Give them a good reason to join and provide great content. You can find articles by LinkedIn experts on the best way to do this. It does work - 80% of my business comes from LinkedIn.

Family It's easy to forget that your family members know and connect with people you don't know or connect with.
1. Reach out and share exactly what you are looking for. Be specific.
2. Ask every quarter so it's stays top of mind.

3. Share with them some of the successes your clients are having as it will make your family feel more comfortable in referring.
4. It's normal for them to be nervous and hesitant because it's their reputation on the line if we mess up.
5. Remember, they know you as a "family" – all your good and not-so-good traits. Deep down they want to see you succeed. Show them that side of you.

This may seem a bit overwhelming when you read the entire book and identify all the actions you need to take.

Take a deep breath. You are in the driver's seat. You can go as slow or as fast as you desire.

The key is to consistently build something new into the system or process you already have. If what you are doing right now isn't working at all, does it need to be tossed? At that point, you'd create a whole new process.

I can't promise you are going to get the same fantastic results as my clients do working privately with me – but I am confident that when you apply and implement what I've shared, your results will improve.

You can do this.

You have something important to offer that others want.

You want to make a difference
.
You deserve the life you dream of.

One last shameless plug: If you'd like to chat with me for clarification on how you can fill your appointment book with those who want, need, and are willing to buy what you offer, sign up for your **free 30-minute strategy session** at **http://timetrade.com/book/D58FP**

No pressure. No obligation. Just great ideas you can apply to help more people and make more sales.

For more content, visit my blog at **www.suehenrytalks.com**

Please be sure to share your successes with me so I can post all about you on my social media channels!

RECOMMENDED RESOURCES

These are tools and sites that I use and recommend. Some include affiliate links which allow me to get paid a bit if someone signs up with that link... However, I'm recommending the tools and sites because I believe in them and use them...

ClickFunnels http://suehenrytalks.com/getmoresales absolute favorite tool to create beautiful lead, sales, thank you pages, etc. I'm not a techie but I found it very easy to use and because I can customize many aspects of them, they don't look like the same thing others are using. I also have my membership site hosted here with my online course, Speak Your Way To Success. The site offers a free 14-day trial period with this link.

Aweber http://suehenrytalks.com/aweber – This is the autoresponder I've used for years and love.

GoToWebinar – If you want to hold group coaching sessions, focus groups, or masterminds, Go To Webinar is the best! (in my humble opinion and I've tried lots of other options!)

Evernote – A complete tool (and life saver) for your crazy life! There is a free version. The Premium is only like $40/annually. Evernote can be added to your smart phone, tablet, and computer. They synch automatically. You can create new notebooks and then write and stores notes under them. When I travel, I add my hotel, shuttle, eticket info, boarding passes, car rental and conference info under 1 notebook. It's all there at a glance and no internet required. Makes it so easy! Visit www.evernote.com

Website Help: Need to either update your current website or create a new one that is mobile friendly? I rely on Carol Lundgreen Lamoreaux. She's fast, easy to work with, patient with non-techies like me, and so affordable! Check her out at www.promomsolutions.com

Book Writing and Marketing: The secret to generating more leads and endless referrals while quickly converting prospects into customers, clients, or patients is to position yourself as a trusted authority. And there's no better way to position yourself as an authority, leap frog over your competition, and catapult your profits than by writing a book.

If you're interested in writing a book to grow your business, then I recommend visiting Weston Lyon's website for more information about writing, publishing, and profiting with a book.

He's a good friend and his material will serve you well: **www.PlugAndPlayPublishing.com**.

SoundCloud – A free online tool to record up to 2 hours of content before needing the paid version. I have my clients record their stories on Sound Cloud and then listen back to them to see how they really sound. It's invaluable – especially if you are counting on your voice and speech to inspire, motivate, and compel others to take action. When you are done, simply delete the recordings you don't want so you can stay below the 2-hour threshold. www.soundcloud.com

Thinkific: Looking for an easy-to-use site to host your online course? Thinkific is great and is easy to figure out, even for nontechies like me. It's not as robust as ClickFunnels but if you are just looking for a place to host content for your program, check it out. There are 3 different payment options – Free, $39/month, and $79/month.
www.suehenrytalks.com/thinkific

10628292R00026

Printed in Great Britain
by Amazon